The Ants and the Grasshopper

All summer long, the ants
were busy in their garden.
First, they dug up the soil.
They raked it and raked it until it was smooth and flat.
As they worked, they sang this song:

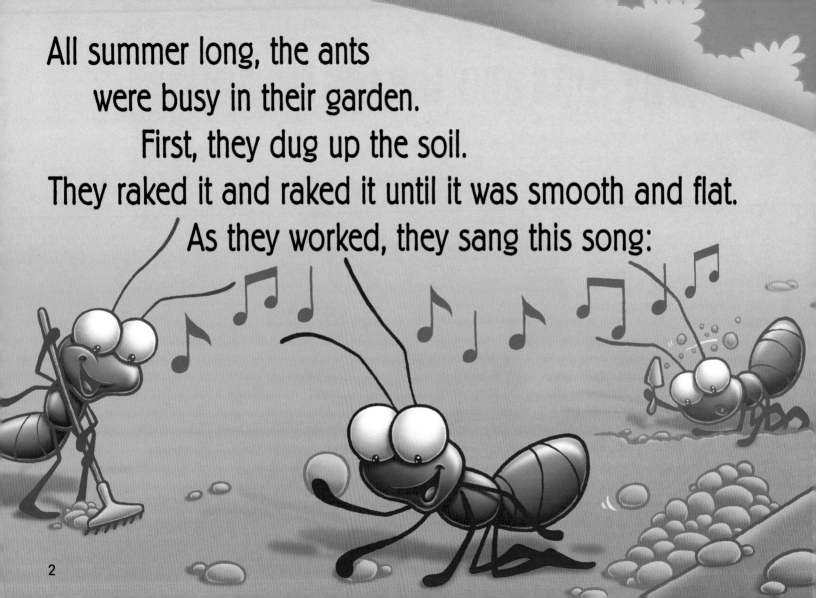

We'll plant the seeds. We'll help them grow.
We'll have plenty of food when the winter winds blow.

The grasshopper saw the ants working
and heard the ants singing.
"Winter?!" said the grasshopper.

"Why think about winter
on a nice summer day like today?
I'll worry about winter later
and have fun today."

4

The ants made little rows in the soil.

Then they planted seeds in each row.

They watered the seeds.

They pulled out weeds.

As they worked, they sang this song:

We'll plant the seeds. We'll help them grow.
We'll have plenty of food when the winter winds blow.

The grasshopper saw the ants working
and heard the ants singing.

The grasshopper turned up his music
and hopped away to the beach with his friends.

"I'll worry about winter later
and have fun today."

BEACH

The garden was growing green and lush.
The ants invited a praying mantis
and ladybug over for lunch.

Those two ate all the bad bugs that were eating the leaves.

The ants watered and weeded and kept the snails away, too.

At the end of summer, the ants picked their crop. They carried the food to the anthill to store it.

When the winter winds came,
the ants crawled into the anthill.
They were as cozy as can be.
They had plenty of food, too.

But the grasshopper was left out in the cold.
He shivered in the cold. He was hungry, too.

The only food he could find was a few seeds
dropped by the ants.
He heard them singing in the anthill . . .

We planted our seeds. We helped them grow.
We have plenty of food. Let the winter winds blow!

And you, dear grasshopper,
did not think ahead.
You played when you should
have been working instead.